South America

Traveling Stories

Won Ho Chang

Prologue

I was once told by my grandfather that my life's destiny came under the sign of the "running horse," and that destiny would one day carry me around the world. The Confucian source of that prophecy, *The Book of*  *Changes*, considered one person's lifespan to be sixty years. I've now surpassed that span by more than two decades, but my destiny keeps me running. Now, as a retiree, I've settled at Laguna Woods Village, in California, but I will continue to travel the world and search for renewed meaning in my life.

What meaning does my life hold for me now? I invite you to join me as I run to explore that question in the pages that follow.

Contents

1 Rio de Janeiro, Brazil

Our cruise on the Star Princess was to start from Buenos Aires, Argentina on the 28th day of February, and we needed to go there by air. Our travel agent advised us to see Rio de Janeiro and the Iguazu Falls in Brazil before we boarded the cruise ship.

On the 23rd day of February, our traveling group of four couples went to Los Angeles airport to go to the beautiful Rio harbor via Miami, Florida.

We arrived at the Rio airport around 9 in the morning of February 24, and were greeted by a Korean travel guide with a very comfortable mini-bus. Our guide did not waste any time and we were immediately off to the first famous place, the gigantic statue of Jesus Christ, which was created between 1922 and 1931.

The statue is 98 feet high, excluding its 26 feet pedestal. The arms stretch 92 feet wide. The statue weighs 635 metric tons, and is located at the peak of the 2,300 feet Corcovado Mountain in the Tijuca Forest National Park overlooking the city of Rio de Janeiro. A symbol of Christianity, the statue has become a cultural icon of Rio de Janeiro and Brazil.

Sugarloaf Cable Car

Then our friendly guide led us to go on the Sugarloaf Cable Car, which moves between Praia Vermelha and the Sugarloaf Mountain. It stops at Morro da Urca on its way up and down, and reaches the summit of the 1,299-foot mountain.

The cableway, according to our guide, was envisioned by the engineer Augusto Ferreira Ramos in 1908 who sought support from well-known figures of Rio's high society to promote its construction. Opened in 1912, it was only the third cableway to be built in the world. In 1972 the cars were updated, growing from a capacity of 22 to 75, and in 1979 it featured in an action scene for the James Bond film *Moonraker*.

Carretao Restaurant

We were tired from flying for around 16 hours and touring this beautiful harbor city and asked our smart guide to take us to the famous restaurant, Carretao, which was in the tour program. But first we checked in to one of beach hotels to take a nap before we went to the restaurant.

Happy Birthday Mrs. Kim!

Located in Ipanema, Carretao sets the standard for Brazilian Style Steakhouses (All you can eat) and fine dining which combines quality, variety and service. Carefully selected ingredients are the key factor in the success of the restaurant. The irresistible menu includes meats of all types, hot dishes, salads, appetizers and a Japanese food buffet.

We were delighted to know that it was Mrs. Kim's birthday and we all celebrated her birthday.

After the wonderful dinner with Brazilian beer, we were booked at 10 that night to see a South American cultural show. We were soaked in Latin American music and dancing the Tango until midnight of the first day in Rio de Janeriro.

Cathedral of Rio de Janeiro

The following day, we were taken to the center of the city, where we toured the Cathedral of Rio de Janeiro, built between 1964 and 1979, and dedicated to Saint Sebastian, the patron saint of Rio de Janeiro.

Cathedral of Rio de Janeiro

With a standing-room capacity of 20 thousand people, its 106 meters internal diameter. In the basement, the Sacred Art Museum has a collection of sculptures, murals, artwork, and fonts used to baptize the princes of the Portuguese royal family.

We also viewed the whole harbor from a touring boat. Rio is a beautiful harbor and very memorable city. Then we were taken to the airport to fly to Iguazu Falls.

2 Iguazu Falls

In front of Devil's Throat

When we arrived in Iguazu Falls airport late in the afternoon, we were led to a Chinese restaurant. After a big dinner, we checked into our hotel.

Our tour guide briefed us about Iguazu Falls, which are waterfalls of the Iguazu River on the border of Argentina and Brazil. Together, they make up the largest waterfall system in the world. The falls divide the river into the upper and lower

Iguazu. The Iguazu River rises near the heart of the city of Curitiba. For most of its course, the river flows through Brazil; however, most of the falls are on the Argentine side.

Beautiful Iguazu Falls

Legend has it that a deity planned to marry a beautiful woman named Naipí, who fled with her mortal lover Tarobá in a canoe. In a rage, the deity sliced the river, creating the waterfalls and condemning the lovers to an eternal fall.

Numerous islands along the 1.7-mile edge divide the Falls into many separate waterfalls and cataracts, varying between 197 to 269 feet high. The number of these smaller waterfalls fluctuates from 150 to 300, depending on the water level. Approximately half of the river's flow falls into a long and narrow chasm called the Devil's Throat, which is U-shaped, 82 meters high, 150 m wide, and 700 m long.

Under the Iguazu Falls

The most memorable experience was a boat ride under the water falls.

Then we drove to the Argentinian side of the Falls to see the Devil's Throat. In one of the widest stretches across the Iguazu River, appears the most important and monumental waterfall of Iguazu cascades system: The Devil's Throat.

The journey begins with about 1,200 yards of footbridges leading to the monumental waterfall, after getting off the Jungle Train at Devil's Throat Station. You can also enjoy the environment that the Iguazu River and its small islands offer, actually a refuge of countless and picturesque deep blue jays.

The bridge leading to the balcony that faces the waterfall is just over 1,200 yards in length, and it is safe and quiet, either by foot or even by wheelchair, as it's absolutely flat. The end of the tour, at the balcony, offers a magical and unique moment, facing a huge wall of water of over 262 feet high, located on the border of Argentina and its sister Brazil.

The Itaipu Dam is a hydroelectric dam on the Parana River located on the border between Brazil and Paraguay. The construction of the dam was first contested by Argentina, but the negotiations and resolution of the dispute ended up setting the basis for Argentine–Brazilian integration later on.

The name "Itaipu" was taken from an isle that existed near the construction site. In the Guarani language, *Itaipu* means "the sounding stone." The Itaipu Dam's hydroelectric power plant produced the most energy of any in the world as of 2016, setting a new world record of

over 100 million megawatt hours, and surpassed
the Three Gorges Dam plant in energy production
in 2015 and 2016.

Completed in 1984, it is a binational
undertaking run by Brazil and Paraguay at the
border between the two countries, 9.3 mile north
of the Friendship Bridge. The installed generation
capacity of the plant is 14 GW, with 20 generating
units providing 700 MW each with a hydraulic
design head of 387 feet.

Of the twenty generator units currently installed, ten generate at 50 Hz for Paraguay and ten generate at 60 Hz for Brazil. Since the output capacity of the Paraguayan generators far exceeds the load in Paraguay, most of their production is exported directly to the Brazilian side.

3 Buenos Aires, Argentina

Colon Theatre

We were happily greeted by a young tour guide, Yune, when we arrived in Buenos Aires airport at two o'clock in the afternoon of February 27, 2019 as arranged by Aju Tour Company in Los Angeles.

The first place MS Yune guided us was to the Colon Theatre, which sets the benchmark for fine acoustics and gilded walls. She told us that this theatre was the first place she showed to tourists who came to this marvelous harbor city. She also proudly told us that we were in the Paris of the Latin America.

The Colon Theater as a Book Store

At the end of the 19th century, according to Yune, Buenos Aires was becoming of the wealthiest and most important cities in the world and to reflect its status, beautiful mansions and buildings reminiscent of Rome, Paris and London were built.

This Colon Theatre is a prime example of German, French and Italian Renaissance styles. Acknowledged as the third best opera house in the world by National Geographic, the old structure is one of the city's most treasured gems and a designated historical monument.

However, I was shocked to see this theatre had become a book store, a book store, which has not been doing well at all here or anywhere. I was only relieved to know that this book store is keeping most of the

Plaza de Mayo

features of the Colon Theatre while wonderfully displaying merchandises of a book store.

Then Yune took us to the Plaza de Mayo and Casa Rosada. Since the revolution of May 25, 1810 that led to Argentine independence, this imposing city square and its Casa Rosada presidential mansion has played a pivotal role in the political life of Buenos Aires.

Metropolitan Cathedral

When we arrived at the plaza, there were a number of political gatherings and our bus was parked a few blocks away. Yune told us that this type of political demonstration goes on every day, and tourists and citizens were not happy with the situation.

We walked to the plaza and toured the Buenos Aires Metropolitan Cathedral, which was located in the city center, overlooking Plaza de Mayo, on the corner of San Martín and Rivadavia streets.

We were tired and asked Yune to take us to a Korean restaurant in the city. The Korean restaurant owner was from Kwangju, a south-western metro politan city of the Korean peninsula, and we were treated with very nice menu of the Kwangju style of cooking.

Flower Park and "Generic Flower"

The second day of our stay in this beautiful harbor city started early in the morning. We quickly toured the Plaza de Mayo, where no political gathering was being held, and moved to the monumental La Flor, a symbol of nature in the middle of the lake in Buenos Aires's "United Nations Flower Park. "The monument was created in 1956 as a tribute for human rights.

UBA School of Law

The park is situated next to the School of Law of the University of Buenos Aires and to the Museum of "Museo de Bellas Artes." In the year 2000, an Argentinean architect Eduardo Catalano donated the gigantic flower called "Generic Flower" to the city of Buenos Aires.

Then we moved to the La Recoleta Cemetery, where the final resting place for Juan and Evita Peron ca be seen. A former church garden dating back 300 years, the cemetery's fanciful array of 6,400 mausoleums are laid out like a city with street names and a town center.

I was so moved to see that there was no destruction of political enemies in this cemetery, unlike in my home country, Korea, where we could not keep a statute of Dr. Syngman Rhee, the first President of the republic.

We still had a few hours before we needed to go to the harbor to board the Star Princess. Yune escorted us to La Boca, the birthplace of spiritual tango of Argentina. We could see and even smell the oldest and most authentic neighborhood of Buenos Aires.

La Recoleta Cemetery

We strolled along the famous Carminito street museum and alley past colorful outdoor art galleries

La Boca street

where artists hawk their paintings and sketches, and the brightly painted woods and corrugated steel homes stand ready to have their picture taken.

We walked into an open street bar to watch a couple performing a wonderful tango dance, and drank local beer for an hour. Sadly, we had to leave this wonderful city, which was able to maintain its rich European heritage while still proudly displaying its Latin American character. From its wide jacaranda-lined boulevards and Old-World architecture to its

dazzling tango shows and famed gauchos, Buenos
Aires is a city of contrast that delights
and excites.

La Boca Street Bar

4 Montevideo, Uruguay

      The first stopover in Uruguay was in the harbor of Montevideo, the capital city where one half of the 3.5 million population of the country live. Our travel agent in California had arranged with a local tour company to do an excursion in the city. We were delighted to meet a young tour guide, Edwardo, with a comfortable mini-bus.

Edwardo started to tell us a bit of the history of Montevideo, which dates back to a colonial dispute between the Spanish and the Portuguese, when the Spanish captured the citadel overlooking the natural harbor in1724.

The Spanish governor of Buenos Aires commanded the settlement of San Felipe de Montevideo two years later as a strategic plan to prevent further Portuguese colonial advancement from Brazil. And in 1828, Montevideo gained the title of the Uruguay's capital just after Uruguay became independent in August 1825. Today, this beautiful city boasts of spaciously tree-lined boulevards, lush parks,

and well-preserved colonial architecture, all exciting to explore.

Edwardo took us to Punta Del Este Ewsort which was a narrow stretch of land which divided the waters of the Atlantic Ocean and the La Plata river. This striking waterfront setting offers stunning beaches with a wide array of amusements and recreational activities for the travelers to sample.

We moved on to see the Solis Theatre which stands at the edge of Plaza Independencia, on the fringe of the Old Town, set back a little from the square and in the block next to the shiny, new Uruguayan Presidency building. It was named for Juan Díaz de Solís, the Spanish navigator who sailed up the River Plate in 1516 and in so doing was the first European to set foot in what is now Uruguay.

We were able to only look at the theater building just looked at the theater building. All of us, however, wished to see a performance in this historically marvelous Opera House.

Edward took us to the lively Marcado del Puerto (Port Market) food court for our lunch, and we found the fresh local cuts of meat, locally created artisan crafts and souvenirs very interesting in this 130-year-old market. I was really tempted to try a dish of barbequed pig on a wood burning fire, but none of our group would join me for the feast.

Independence Plaza

Then we went to Plaza Indepencia, or Independence Square. Known for its superb building design, this central Plaza separates the older Cludad Vieja from the more modern downtown Montevideo.

Our tour guide, Edwardo, spoke about his country all the time we were driving around the city. He was very proud of his country as a successful model of socialism. A resident of Montevideo can rent a house for about $50, but their income tax rate is about 36% and sales tax was 22 %.

Edward also spoke about their former President, Jose Mujica, who served as President (2010–15) after being long imprisoned for his guerrilla activities with a revolutionary organization. Mujica listed a 1987 Volkswagen as his total asset, and stayed in his small house while the Presidential mansion was given to home-less people. He also donated 87% of his salary to the government. He still lives in his own house and drives the 1987 Volkswagen. Edwardo and Uruguayan love this legendary former president.

While listening to Edwardo's story, we arrived at the Monumento la Carreta, which was created by a local sculptor Jose Belloni, in honor of the ox-cart drivers of the 19th century. The granite sculpture was first installed in 1934, and was recently restored by the artist's grandson. It is recognized as a National Historic Monument.

Before we returned to the Star Princess, Edwardo proudly explained Estadio Centenario, which is used primarily for soccer. The stadium was built between 1929 and 1930 to host the inaugural 1930 FIFA World Cup, as well as to commemorate the centennial of Uruguay's first constitution. According

to Edwardo, Uruguay won the first FIFA championship
by beating the Argentinian team 4-2.

5 Puerto Madryn, Argentina

When we arrived at the beautiful but windy Madryn harbor early in morning, our tour guide was waiting for our group of 16 people with a four-wheel drive restructured bus. The guide, then, told us we were going to Punta Tombo which is one of the most famous and visited sites in the Argentinian Patagonian coast.

Thousands of tourists gather here to be amazed at one of the most fascinating shows performed by nature: the Magellanic penguin continental colony. About two million Magellanic penguins gather there from September to April in order to nest, mate, incubate their eggs and feed their offspring.

We left Puerto Madryn heading southwards along National Route 3 and, after traveling 70 km, we took unpaved Provincial Route 1, which led us to Punta Tombo after three hours of rough driving for 107 km. When we arrived at the reserve, we let ourselves be carried away by the endless vision of thousands of penguins which were looking for their nests here and there.

Magellanic Penguin

The guide explained that the venue where the reserve is located used to belong to Estancia La Perla, and that it had been donated by Luis and Francisco La Regina. The aim of this reserve is to protect one of the most diverse sea bird colony in Argentina and the largest Magellanic penguin continental colony, providing for almost two million penguins.

As we approached the very point after which this place is named, amidst the typical arid and desolate Patagonian steppe, we observed a surprising activity. There we saw a rocky 3-km-long and 600-meter-wide mass getting into the sea, covered by sand, clay, and gravel and surrounded by large sandy beaches. This beach lodges the largest concentration of sea birds in the entire Patagonian littoral. The offspring area is concentrated in the sandy lands located at the base of the point.

On the half way back to the harbor, there was a huge stone-age dinosaur monument, which reminded us that this area had been occupied by Tehuelche Indians and was the site of the charming town of

Trelew. Trelew offeres a menagerie of architectural delights and a mixture of different cultures and religions.

The rough riding in an uncomfortable jeep for six hours to Punta Tombo had drained our energy, but our brilliant cruise director arranged many entertaining programs on the ship to help us recover from the excursion.

We were amazed to see a Tango performance by a couple in the Piazza area of the ship, while we sipped a tasty margarita drink. We were very nostalgic to think back on our times, when we had enjoyed the Tango dancing some years ago.

.

6 Falkland Island

     The Falkland Islands lie between the Antarctic and South American continent in the South Atlantic Ocean about 8,000 miles from Britain. During the 18th Century, the British Empire retained only these small islands while the Spanish and the Portuguese dominated the whole South American hemisphere.

I remembered vaguely about the 1982 Falkland War. I had to read writings of Lawrence Freedman, official historian of the Falklands War. I thought the war was a ridiculous event of colonial fighting in the 20th Century.

Gypsy Cove

According to Lawrence Freedman, on 2 April 1982, Argentina invaded the Falkland Islands, a remote British colony in the South Atlantic. The UK, which had ruled the islands for nearly 150 years (though Argentina had long claimed sovereignty), quickly chose to fight: Britain's Navy sailed south to retake the Falklands. After a series of engagements, the Argentinian forces surrendered on 14 June.

The war cost some 650 Argentine and 253 British dead and did not settle the dispute: Argentina still claims the Falklands. If it had left well alone in 1982, concluded Freedman, depopulation would eventually have left the Falklands unviable. Instead the victory led to firmer British commitment, and so the

Gypsy Cove

Falklands is more prosperous and secure than ever before.

Established by the British in 1485, Port Stanley, capital of the Falklands, became successful as a deep-water port specializing in repairs for ships traveling through the Straights of Magellan on their way to California 's Gold Rush.

As one of the busiest ports, Stanley has been its share of nautical disasters. We could see the hulls of 20 ships destroyed by the North Atlantic's treacherous storms.

The pristine beaches and crystal blue waters of the Falkland's teem with hundreds of species of wild life, and gentoo penguins are the most famous animal inhabitants of the sea. We took one of local tour buses to go to the Gypsy Cove. It was a relatively short bus

ride from downtown to Gypsy Cove for us to enjoy the sights.

We saw a large number of penguins as well a number of other birds, and sea life. We also saw the Star Princess anchored in the bay as well. These islands have some of largest rockhopper penguin colonies in the world. Standing only 20 inches tall and weighing in at around five pounds, rockhoppers are the smallest penguins but they are definitely most agile. They are hopping from their perch on the rocky cliffs to jumping in the water looking for food then hopping back up the rocks to feed their young baby birds.

It was a cold and windy day in the Falklands. But three couples of our group went to see Kelp Point, where there is a growing elephant seal colony and one of the most scenic areas of the islands.

Kelp Point

7 Cape Horn, Chile

Cape Horn is the southernmost headland of the Tierra del Fuego archipelago of southern Chile, and is located on the small Hornos Island. Although not the most southerly point of South America (which are the Diego Ramírez Islands), Cape Horn marks the northern boundary of the Drake Passage and marks where the Atlantic and Pacific Oceans meet.

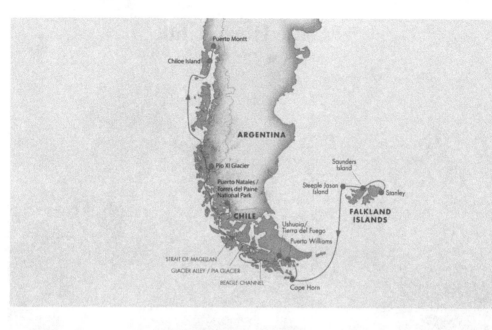

Cape Horn was discovered and first rounded in 1616 by the Dutchman Willem Schouten, who named it after the city of Hoorn in the Netherlands. For decades, Cape Horn was a major milestone on the clipper route, by which sailing ships carried trade around the world.

The need for boats and ships to round Cape Horn was greatly reduced by the opening of the Panama Canal in August 1914. However, sailing around the Cape Horn is still widely regarded as one of the major challenges in yachting.

Thus a few recreational sailors continue to sail this route, sometimes as part of a circumnavigation of the globe. Almost all of these choose routes through the channels to the north of the Cape.

The waters around Cape Horn are particularly hazardous, owing to strong winds, large waves, strong currents and icebergs; these dangers have made it notorious as a sailors' graveyard.

The Star Princess stayed a distance from the Cape Horn for an hour, but close enough to see the island. It was cold and windy as usual so that we just took a few pictures and moved back inside the ship. Later we received a certificate of rounding Cape Horn.

Captain Tuvo, then, hosted a formal dinner on the night and served a very special lobster-tail dish. For the formal dinner, ladies and gentlemen wore their special dresses and tuxedoes. Photographers from the crew set up many studio-type settings for us to take our pictures.

After that very special dinner by our captain, we were entertained with a musical show to celebrate the legendary Whitney Houston, who was born in 1963 and died in 2012 at her age of 48. This superbly entertaining concert was well received by senior passengers like us.

We were emotionally drenched so much with our nostalgic memory that we went up to the sky lounge for drinks after the show. Mr. and Mrs. Lee, one couple of our group had taken the 110-day world cruise of the Princess line the year before and had received a very prestigious Elite Captain's Circle membership, and we were able to use the 17th deck Sanctuary lounge for drinks.

8 Ushuaia, Argentina

Ushuaia is nestled in a U-shaped cove adjacent to the dazzling Beagle Channel, offering the curious traveler myriad visual delights at every turn. Its backdrop of beech trees and towering mountains has" a distinct adventurous appeal that will beckon us to explore and discover," according a port guide from the Star Princess.

It is hard to believe that this travel gem was once a former penal colony, but this city owes its very existence to that historical event because inmates constructed the town's railway, hospital and port.

Today, Ushuaia is our gateway to a rugged wilderness of a natural beauty. When the prison closed its door in 1947, Ushuaia had a meager population of about 3,000 inhabitants. Fast-forward to the current day, and Ushuaia's population has steadily grown to a metropolis of around 70,000 residents, quadrupling in size during the 70'ss and 80's.

When we arrived in the Ushuaia port early in the morning, we were greeted by a tour guide of a private tour company with a sightseeing bus. We started the tour driving towards the Tierra del Fuego National Park the southernmost Argentinian National Park. This was the route to reach Lapataia Bay, the last kilometer on the earth, located on the "Panamericana" route, officially known as "the end of the world."

Once there, we were surrounded by an incredible ecosystem and the feeling of having reached the last possible place accessible with wheels. Within the national park we visited two "must see" places for pictures; Roca Lake and Ensenada Zaratieguí. We continued our tour leaving the park, still on the Panamericana road, going towards the northeast region. We drove entire route in a wonderful journey of incredible landscapes, to reach panoramic points and take photos. On the way, we stopped at the winter center and then came back to the harbor.

Onboard once more, we looked over the Pipo River, and its sylvan valley in addition to a myriad of waterfalls, forests, mountains and rivers. We were heading to the Ensenada Bay that affords magnificent views of the Beagle Channel, which was named after the ship that carried Charles Darwin.

9 Punta Arenas, Chile

Practically the southernmost town in Chile, Punta Arenas is a mishmash of corrugated-iron-roofed buildings, a busy port, and a small but steadily growing population, boosted by an upturn in the local oil industry. Facing the Strait of Magellan, it's often battered by freezing southerlies and has a colonist backstory. It started out as a settlement created by Captain John Williams, a seaman from Bristol working for the Chileans. It moved to its present site in 1848, and an English sailor named it 'Sandy Point' (Punta Arenas).

After a brief period as an unsuccessful penal colony, Punta Arenas expanded during the late 19th-century wool boom and attracted many immigrants, mainly from Britain and the Balkans.

Punta Arenas has been Chile's doorway to Antarctic exploration since the days of Robert Falcon Scott. Today, it's also a major port for cruises into the icy reaches of Tierra del Fuego, and a gateway for fly-cruises to Antarctica. A drab town in many ways, it does have some notable monuments strewn along its waterfront, which the Avenida Costanera del Estrecho and 21 de Mayo roads run along.

They include a replica of Ferdinand Magellan's tall ship, Victoria, and the rusting remains of the shipwrecked Lord Lonsdale, an English frigate that now serves as a de facto monument to all seafaring explorers.

Punta Arenas is very much a place of transition. Unless you wish to visit the penguin colony, we recommend simply staying for a night after your flight here, before continuing your onward journey to Torres del Paine National Park in Chilean Patagonia. A city tour introduced us not only to the local history but the classic style of life of people in a faraway region called Patagonia.

This tour started in Plaza de Armas and paused to admire the European buildings lining the city center and the statue honoring the discoverer of the Strait of Magellan in 1520 which linked the Atlantic and the Pacific.

Downtown streets off the Plaza de Armas sold handmade wood carvings, stoneware from local artisans and knitwear. It was a short drive up to Cerro de la Cruz, where we could wander over to enjoy the great view where the city draws cruises and we could see the mysterious and captivating Island of Tierra del Fuego.

After a ten minutes photo-stop overlooking the city and we headed towards the beautiful promenade to enjoy an amazing speech about history and the geology of the area. Then we drove to the well worth visiting museum known as Nao Victoria, where we will find a recreation of the ship in which Magellan navigated and discovered the Strait.

National Monument Cemetery

We also toured the National Monument Cemetery, which was not only for the architecture and impressive mausoleums. but walking amongst the perfect lined tall cypress trees brought from Europe in the 19th Century.

10 Amalia Glacier, Chile

Amalia Glacier

Back on the ship, we were reminded repeatedly that it would be around four in the afternoon when we would reach the Amalia Glacier, which was also popularly known as the Skua Glacier. Right after a quick lunch, we were positioned on the 16th deck to see and take pictures. It was cold with a harsh wind in the open area of the ship, but the scenery around the canals and the Rocky Mountains kept us staying there anyway.

The glaciers' origin can be traced to the Southern Patagonian Ice Field. From the year 1945 to 1986, the terminus retreated about 7 km together with the recession of the O'Higgins Crater, which is regarded as the most dramatic glacier retreat of the ice field during the time.

About 10,000 years ago the Patagonian Ice Field covered a major fraction of Southern Chile. In this day and age, the region paves the way to the islands and channels that make up the fjords of the Pacific Coast of Southern Chile which extend to the Strait of Magellan and Tierra del Fuego. It is a tidewater glacier that is located in the Bernardo O'Higgins National Park. The glacier is known to surround the Reclus volcano and erodes the northern side of it.

The Star Princess moved slowly down the canal which ends with the Amalia Glacier. It was pretty neat to see but the ship was a lot further from a glacier than it was during an Alaskan cruise. The ship crept up to the point of "best viewing" and we were able to see it all from the front top side of the ship.

About the time of departure, we went back to our stateroom to change for dinner at 5:30. During dinner and the night, we finished sailing about 75 miles in the open ocean and the ship turned west into the Estrecho de Magallanes (known to us as the Strait of Magellan).

This is an inland passageway between the Atlantic and the Pacific. This passage cuts off about

200 sea-miles for ships rather than going all the way around the tip of Cape Horn, and would have spared those early sailors a very difficult passage. For our ship it meant smoother sailing all through the night. It also led us to tomorrow's port city, Puerto Montt.

After dinner our group went to the Princess Theater for the show. The performer in the theater was the same singer/instrumentalist which I had seen two before. I stayed in the Piazza and watched a little of the dancing demonstration, a couple doing the Tango. They were very good.

11   Puerto Montt, Chile

After sailing a day and two nights, we arrived in Puerto Montt on March 11, 2019. The site that is currently this charming harbor town was once layered in dense forest. We marveled at the multitude of snow-capped volcanoes interspersed with charming alpine valleys surrounded by rolling hills.

The city was once a nexus for German immigrants to occupy, hence the "German Village" we found among Puerto Varas manicured rose gardens.

Puerto Montt

The quaint town of Puerto Vara was established by German immigrants 150 years ago. Situated on the edge of Lake Llanquihue, Puerto Vara is an excellent showcase of German architecture and food.

Puerto Varas

    During the tour, we saw the contour of the lake while its crystal-clear waters accompanied each of our movements, as if it were another passenger in the tour.

    Puerto Varas is an excellent starting point in a full-day land circuit around Lake Llanquihue, covering every nook. For such purpose, we left behind the eye-catching German architecture of the city in order to slowly enter wilder areas and get deep into the Valdivian rainforest.

German style Church

We set out from the downtown following the road leading to Ensenada to the East. In a few minutes, we had left away from the populated area. We passed the beaches known as Hermosa, Niklitscher, Punta

Cabras and Poza Loreley, each of them featuring a particular kind of charm.

We drove along the Petrohue River which offered a joyous array of outdoor adventures of fishing, whitewater rafting and kayaking.

When we reached the cascading waters at Petrohue Falls, we could not stop taking pictures of this breath-taking scenery. We moved into the majesty of the Vincente Perez National Park, where we could view the towering evergreen trees, as well as the fascinating three active volcanoes: Tronador, Puntiagudo and Osorno.

Petrohue River

The waterfall was supported by basaltic lava stemming from the Osorno Volcano that sat in between Todos los Santos and Llanquihue Lake and provides an interesting background for pictures. The water, decanted in the lake, is usually clear with a green hue; however, occasionally, when lava descend from the volcano when it is active, water at the falls can be loaded with sand and silt. Transport of these abrasive materials explains the polished aspect of the rocks.

Osorno Volcano is particularly noteworthy due to its lofty apex rising over 8,700 feet into the sky. This titan Fujiyama of South America is one of the most well-known active volcanoes in the Southern Chilean Andes.

12 San Antonio, Chile

San Antonio is a new port to cruises. The Princess Line also changed its dock from Valparaiso to San Antonio. We were recommended by the excursion staff to try the variety of fish and Chilean wine, and to visit the Pablo Neruda museum in San Antonio.

The cruise port of San Antonio is about 70 miles west of Santiago. For this reason, many cruisers chose to go to Santiago, the energetic capital city of Chile. Santiago is a great city to simply stroll around as each of its neighborhoods has a distinct personality.

Since we had visited Santiago and Valparaiso 2011, we stayed in San Antonio, and enjoyed a tour of some of its surrounding historical areas. San Antonio has picturesque fishing ports and beautiful sea views of Chile's Pacific coast. On the seaside of the city of San Antonio there is a walk called The Beautiful Sea Walk, which includes a mall and the Casino of the Pacific, where watched the merchant ships, and the activities of fishermen and the port workers.

Valparaíso Coast

Valparaíso is one of the country's most important seaports and a cultural center of the Southwest Pacific. Valparaíso played an important geopolitical role in the second half of the 19th century when the city served as a major stopover for ships crossing the Straits of Magellan while traveling between the Atlantic and Pacific oceans.

Valparaíso Harbor

The harbor grew quickly during its golden age, and the city eventually became known by international sailors as "Little San Francisco." However, the opening of the Panama Canal and resulting loss of ship traffic was a staggering blow to Valparaíso, though the city has undergone an impressive renaissance in recent years.

A nice German-made bus and a guide from a Korean travel agency were waiting for us when we moved out of the port terminal. We were then treated to a tour of the harbor, which looked just like a Spanish port of 19th century. We also visited the Veramonte winery on the way to Santiago.

Veramonte winery

The winery is located in a valley with a diversity of microclimates. The valley floor's cool climate is ideal for growing Chardonnay. The foothills are warmer, similar to the northern reaches of the Napa Valley, and the climate is suited to Bordeaux grape that have become the basis of Primus, an exotic Chilean blend.

Veramonte's Casablanca vineyard produces lower yields than other grape growing regions in Chile, resulting in grapes with a greater intensity and concentration. As a tourist spot, the winery charged $8.00 to tour the facility, and a glass of wine cost $4.00, which was more than we paid at any restaurant in Valparaiso.

La Moneda Palace

Santiago is Chile's political and cultural center, and its central location makes it a great base for visiting other areas. It's a fast-growing city between the Andes mountain range to the east and the Cordillera to the west.

We had a full-day tour of this wonderful city of six million, starting from the La Moneda Palace, where the office of the president of Chile and its cabinet ministries are located, and moving on to the Plaza de Armas, where the biggest and oldest Catholic cathedral in Chile has been preserved. There were many dogs running around the streets of Santiago, so we had to be careful where we stepped.

While we were wandering the palace, we actually met the president, who was coming to his office with a group of secret service staff. He shook our hands in front of the cheering public in front of his office. It was beautiful to see a democratic system at work, even as pictures of violence were being broadcast daily from Egypt.

With President of Chile

We visited the Central Market, where all kinds of fresh fish and vegetables were sold, and we had lunch at a Chilean barbeque restaurant, including a local wine that cost only $10.00 a bottle—the same wine that would have cost $30.00 on the ship. After lunch, we had quite a workout as we made our way to the top of the Santa Lucia, which was similar to the peaks of Hong Kong, except that we had to walk up the long steep hill to see the top of the castle.

Central Market

As the last part of our South American trip, we took a tour bus about a hundred miles to the Portillo Ski Resort in the Andes, the world's longest continental mountain range. The bus driver was cautious as we made our way along a winding mountain road for three hours, but we were treated to wonderful views on both sides of the road.

Inca Lake

When we arrived at the resort, we were please to find no crowds because it was the summer season. We walked down to Laguna de los Incas (Incan Lake), where we heard a legend concerning the last princess of the Incan empire, who took her life in the water. We also had a great lunch featuring traditional Chilean empanadas de Pino, filled with a seasoned mixture of ground beef, onions, raisins, black olives, and hard-boiled eggs.

We were close to the Argentine border and had to hurry back to prepare for our flight back home. Although Chile is poised to become the richest nation in South America, they need to emphasize globali zation, just as Korean president Y.S. Kim chose it as a top priority. It's simply a good business strategy. We had severe difficulty communicating with most of the service personnel we met in Chile. They simply said "I speak no English" and that was that.

I also noticed many new Kia and Hyundai cars on the streets, since Chile signed a free trade agreement with South Korea some time ago. I was so delighted to see that, and I knew that part of the reciprocal agreement brought inexpensive Chilean wines into South Korea. In my opinion, it would be in everyone's interest for the United States and Korea to work out a similar free trade agreement. I believe it would do better than harm.

13 La Serena (Coquimbo), Chile

We arrived in the Coquimbo harbor early in the morning of March 15, 2019, and wanted to see Choros islands and La Serena. But we did not reserve the sightseeing excursion from the Star Princess.

As we walked outside the harbor, we encountered many private travel agents. We were lucky to hire an agent with his uncle as his driver of a Mercedes van. And we headed north on the Pan-

American Highway and crossed a semi-desert like area.
The road continued on a sloping ground from where we
could observe several views of the rocky coast.

After traveling 80 miles, we arrived at Los
Choros Fishermen's Wharf, a natural viewpoint to see
Gaviota, Choro and Damas Islands.

We were asked to board a motor launch leading
us to Humboldt Penguins National Reserve, which is
part of this area. But we decided to go back to La

Serena, because it was cold and windy, and we did not have enough time for sightseeing La Serena.

Los Choros Fishermen's Wharf

When we arrived in La Serena, our tour guide led us to the University of La Serena, and briefed us about the university, which has five campuses: three in La Serena, one in Coquimbo, and one in Ovalle. It was founded in 1981, and approximately 8,000 students are currently enrolled there. The university was formed via the fusion of two regional campuses of the nationwide

state universities, Universidad de Chile and Uni
versidad Tecnica del Estado.

Then, we moved down to the center of the city
and visited La Recova Municipal Market. The market
place was buzzing the day we visited. There were
people everywhere who were shopping and listening to
some local entertainers sing and playing their guitars
incredibly well. The stalls were mainly tourist oriented
but also for locals who had beautiful fresh flowers on
offer.

Our guide suggested a local restaurant in the market for our lunch, but we were very hesitant to try local foods after being cautioned by the crew of the ship. We ate our packed lunches with local beer that was really good and inexpensive.

La Recova Municipal Market

When travelling in South America, the guide advised us that we always go to the Plaza de Armas in every town we visit. They seem to be the hub of every community. The Plaza de Armas in La Serena is no different. La Serena lays claim to being the second oldest city in Chile. This small and neat park has seating and shade, statuary and a fountain. Bordering the park are the Cathedral, the main pedestrian mall with shops, and some impressive buildings noted for their different styles of architecture from over the years.

The Plaza de Armas in La Serena

Our friendly guide suggested that we move on to the next place, the Monumental Lighthouse, which was built between 1950 and 1951. The building stands tall on the beach of the resort town, but we didn't see any swimmers, only a few merchants selling souvenirs.

Monumental Lighthouse

On our way to go back to Coquimbo, we found many seashore condominium buildings with for sale signs, and the guide asked us if we had any interest in buying one of these resort homes for investment. But we told him we were too old to do such things.

Our friendly guide proudly explained that Chile was among South America's most economically prosperous and socially stable a nations, with a high-income and high living standard.

When we arrived at the Fuerte Lambert, we were amazed to a natural setting with rocks and flowers just like it was in the 17th century.

Fuerte Lambert

Third Millennium Cross Monument

We finally arrived at the Third Millennium Cross Monument, which could be seen from everywhere, even from the coasts of neighboring towns.

It is the highest and most marvelous building work erected in South America in honor of the 2,000 years since the birth of Jesus.

Its base is made of three leaning pillars which form a large tripod. Upon it, the immense Cross made of three columns representing the Holy Trinity is erected. Its maximum height is 83 meters and it is 40 meters wide. The 2,000-step staircase is the access to the base and the worship area, which consists of a chapel, a museum and a photographic exhibition where different stages of the construction of the Cross can be seen, until its inauguration, in May 5th, 2000.

The last stretch up to the vantage point located inside the horizontal arms of the Cross may be visited by taking the elevators or the stairs inside the pillars.

From the large windows of the Cross an amazing 360°
panoramic view of Coquimbo, its bay and the Pacific
Ocean can be appreciated.

Walking along its interior, we noticed a solemn
atmosphere and only soft murmurs could be heard.
Two rooms appear in the arms of the Cross: one of
them keeps the busts of the Chilean Archbishops
during last century, while the other one shows the busts
of Popes John Paul II and Benedict XVI.

After a very impressive tour of the city of La Serena and Coquimbo harbor, we were heading to Pisco, a newly developing harbor of Peru. We had hoped to see Arica in Chile, but the northern harbor of Chile was not in the schedule.

14 Pisco (San Martin), Peru

Tambo Colorado

When we arrived at the Pisco harbor, we were surprised to see a new development of the port. There was no building completed around the port, and constructions of a new harbor town and facilities were going on.

Pisco Haebor

Those who had purchased expensive excursion packages of the Princess could take sightseeing buses in the port. But those who wanted to take a private tour were taken to a small town, Paracas, by bus for about 40 minutes.

We were advised by our friends who had traveled this area to take a private tour which would be better for us. When we arrived in the center of Paracas, we were surrounded by agents of many private tour companies.

We were very lucky to find a couple, the wife as a sales person and the husband as driver of a van, offering a package of seeing the Ballestas Islands and Tambo Colorado.

Paracas Civic Center

After agreeing on terms and conditions, we were guided to the dock of a speedboat to go to the Ballestas Islands, which are an iconic Peruvian sight, but they can only be seen from a tour boat. Among the islands' usual inhabitants, which you may spot on this tour, are penguins, sea lions, and Peruvian boobies.

Along the way, we enjoyed the view of the

mysterious candelabra carved into the hillside. If you visit, you could offer your own theory as to its unknown origin.

We were so impressed and delighted to see these wonderful Ballestas Islands. Then we came back to the town of Paracas and met our driver. We drove about two hours to arrive at the site of the Inca settlement, archaeological museum, Tambo Colorado.

It was most likely built at the end of the 15th century and was ruled by the Inca Emperor Pachacutec.

It is believed that Tambo Colorado was used as an administrative/ceremonial and military place to control the main road from the coast to the highlands. Also, this place was to service as a resting place for the Inca general and his army across the Inca territory.

The site consists of several structure around a large central plaza. The central plaza is shaped like a trapezoid with its largest side being 150m long. The main structures are grouped together in a northern and southern Palaces, plus some ceremonial platforms. Because of local environmental conditions, many of the buildings original colors have been preserved, helping experts reconstruct the site.

Tambo Colorado

15 Lima (Callao), Peru

When we visited Callao harbor in 2011, there was some distance of 10 miles to go to Lima, the capital of Peru, so we were surprised this time to see these two cities are completely connected.

Our tour bus went to Plaza Mayor first. Plaza Mayor, formerly Plaza de Armas, is the heart and birthplace of Lima. The crown jewel of the city, this UNESCO World Heritage–listed square is flanked by many important buildings, such as the Government Palace (Palacio de Gobierno), Cathedral of Lima, City Hall, and the Archbishop's Palace.

Palacio de Gobierno

Cathedral of Lima

The Government Palace of **Peru,** also known as House of Pizarro, was the house of the Peruvian government headquarters and was built over a huge Indian burial ground, Waka, that had a shrine to the last of Indian chief, Taulichusco. It has been through many alterations. The current structure was built in the 20th century, designed by Peru's dictators in the style of grandiose French Baroque architecture.

A Prayer in the Cathedral of Lima

We toured the inside of the Lima Cathedral. Our tour guide started his briefing of this historical cathedral. Construction began in 1535, and the building has undergone many reconstructions and transformations since. It retains its colonial structure and facade. It is dedicated to St John, the Apostle and Evangelist.

There are 14 side chapels, In the left aisle, the first chapel holds the ancient baptistery. Here can be seen a beautiful image of Nuestra Señora de la Esperanza, who presides over the events during Lent and Holy Week. During a recent restoration, ancient pictures were found in this chapel that have been restored and are displayed again for the public.

The next chapel is chapel of the Holy Family, featuring figures of Jesus, Mary and Joseph. The Basilica Cathedral of Lima is also home to the tomb of Francisco Pizarro

Our guide, then, ushered us to a beautiful library nearby the plaza. A formal train station has been converted to a library, which has many historical collections. I was interested to see an old printing press, which was set up in the lobby of the library.

Lima Library

Miraflores is an exclusive residential and upscale shopping district south of downtown Lima. It is also one of the most affluent districts that make up the city of Lima. It has various hotels, restaurants, bars, nightclubs, and department stores.

Miaflores Park

The district is full of hotels, cafés, pubs, restaurants and shops, which draw large crowds of the local population on Sundays. Parque Kennedy,

Miraflores' central plaza, regularly has flea markets and art exhibitions.

Larcomar Shopping Mall

Larcomar, a shopping mall overlooking the Pacific coast, is located in Miraflores, and is very popular among tourists, young people, and the middle and upper classes. There are restaurants, stores, a food court, ice cream shops, arcades, bowling alleys, nightclubs, bars, and the most modern cinema in Lima.

After leaving Lima to reach Puntarenas of Costa Rica, the Star Princess sailed 2 days and nights. During this voyage, we crossed the Equator Line and captain Tuvo and his crews had an Equator Ceremony, as announced many times.

Staying on the ship for 2 days provided me a great time to write my traveling stories while sitting on a beach chair around the Lido swimming pool on the 14th deck. But others also used the two tracks of 298 M on the 7th and 15th decks for their routine exercises.

Walking on the 7th Deck

And there were a number of other exercise programs including sports dance, Yoga practice and Zumba.

Zumba Time

16 Equator Ceremony

After leaving Lima for Puntarenas, Costa Rica, the Star Princess was sailing for three days and nights. At noon of March 22, our friendly captain repeatedly announced that there would be an "Equator Ceremony," that we could not miss, and we all were gathered around the Lido swimming pool on the 14th deck.

Sea travel in general is a deeply traditional practice, with rituals dating back centuries, many of which are still practiced today, even on passenger cruise ships.

One such example is the King Neptune Ceremony, or line-crossing ceremony which traditionally occurs on any cruise ship crossing the Equator. It is a virtual certainty anybody who takes part in a world cruise or even joins a one-way cruise on a ship moving to another part of the world will witness one for themselves.

To start off the ceremonies, all the passengers become "the Pollywogs," so called for being initiates who have crossed the equator for the first time.

For their crimes, the Pollywogs are subjected to a serious of "humiliating" punishments for the amusement of the assembled crowd. In my case, my crime of "having limited French linguistic skills," which resulted in a four-pronged sentence which saw me arm crawling across a tarp covered in dishwashing liquid – my comical struggle for propulsion was met with laughter from the crowd. I also had to do Kissing Neptune's Feet, which meant kissing a fish for good luck and finally crossing the line by swimming under a rope in the ship's pool, which marked the end of my penance.

It was actually an enjoyable experience celebrating the milestone of crossing the Equator and a must for anyone looking for a fun way to pass the afternoon – even if watching from the sidelines.

Although if you plan to participate, I would suggest packing an old swimsuit, as Neptune's punishments, particularly on voyages with a young demographic onboard, can be messy!

Victims are singing YMCA

The next day, we received a certificate for crossing the Equator.

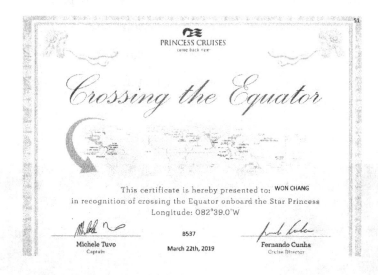

17 Puntarenas, Costa Rica

This visit to Puntarenas is our third adventure in this beautiful area. The first trip to this harbor was in 2011, when we were on a cruise to Santiago, Chile, and flew back to home. This time we chose to go to the town of Grecia.

Grecia lies at an elevation of 999 meters above sea level in the foothills of the Cordillera Central on the eastern edge of the Central Valley.

This highland town is the home of the first toucan to receive a prosthetic beak, named Grecia because of the name of this city where the bird was found injured prior to its admission to the Rescue Institute at Zoo Ave, south of the city.

Iglesias de la Nuestra Señora de las Mercedes

Grecia is also noted for its unique church, Iglesias de la Nuestra Señora de las Mercedes, made entirely of pre-fabricated steel plates painted red. There are several urban legends about this church. One recounts how the church was donated by some foreign country, and sent to Greece as a gift, but was wrongly shipped to Grecia, Costa Rica.

Another legend states that the final destination of the church was the city of Punta Arenas in Chile but was disembarked, by mistake, in the port of Puntarenas, Costa Rica and later sent to the city of Grecia where it was assembled.

However, records clearly show that the instruction, shipment, and construction of the church were a coordinated effort of the Costa Rican government and Alejo E. Jiménez Bonnefil (1858-1922), a Costa Rican coffee producer and exporter who was in charge of importing the church from Belgium in the late 19th Century.

Grecia Coffee Farm

Coffee has played a pivotal role in the development of Costa Rica. It has shaped social, cultural and political institutions and is still one of country's major agricultural exports.

During the second visit to Puntarenas, we toured the Tarcoles River, which is formed by the convergence of two rivers, the Virilla and the Grande de San Ramon, and empties into the Pacific Ocean. In total, the river's watershed covers over 2,000 km. It forms the northern border of the Carara Biological Reserve, and helps irrigate important agricultural areas of the country. In addition to its agricultural significance, the river also helps generate electricity. It is, however, not a good place to swim, as it is highly polluted.

Tarcoles River

During the second visit to Puntarenas, we toured the Tarcoles River is formed by the convergence of two rivers, the Virilla and the Grande de San Ramon, and empties into the Pacific Ocean. In total, the river's watershed covers over 2000 km. It forms the northern border of the Carara Biological Reserve, and helps irrigate important agricultural areas of the country. In addition to its agricultural significance, the river also helps generate electricity. It is, however, not a good place to swim, as it is highly polluted.

The river is perhaps best known for its abundance of American crocodiles. It's said that the Tárcoles River has one of the highest populations of crocodiles in the entire world - 25 crocodiles per square kilometer. Several tour operators take advantage of this fact by offering river tours that guarantee croc sightings. Much of the time these large reptiles can be spotted swimming through the river or sunbathing along the banks.

In addition to the crocodiles, the river also supports more than 50 species of migratory, native and coastal birds, including a variety of heron and egrets, crested caraccas, roseate spoonbills, scarlet macaws and more. Iguanas can often be spotted scampering about the sides of the river as well.

Gondola in Rain Forest

We also toured Rainforest Adventures Costa Rica Pacific, an ecotourism reserve that encompasses 222 acres of transitional rain forest. We enjoyed the scenic ride to the reserve, where we met our expert guides.

We were taken to an open-air gondola for a 1-hour aerial tram ride that looked through all levels of the rain forest. As we glided through the trees, our naturalist guide pointed out native flora and fauna, such as capuchin monkeys, sloths, toucans, blue morpho butterflies and hummingbirds.

The gentle ride took us up as high as 130 feet for sweeping views of the forest below and the Pacific Ocean in the distance.

Hot Spring Pool in Baldi Hotel

During our third visit, we took an option to go to Baldi Hot Springs, which are a hundred percent natural and rich in mineral salts and ions such as magnesium, calcium and chlorine as they come from the underground sources of Arenal Volcano.

Hot Spring Pool in Baldi Hotel

Hot springs are designed in a way that will make us feel they are in a natural thermal river in the middle of the rainforest. Thermal water is naturally heated by the Arenal Volcano and its underground rivers. The waters don't need any pumping or drilling but can reach the pools with the force of gravity. It was very impressive.

18 San Juan Del Sur, Nicaragua

When we arrived at San Juan del Sur, we were surprised to see the harbor was not fully developed to handle big cruise ships. The Star Princess was anchored far away from the beach, and passengers were transported by boats used for emergency situation.

When we hired a tour guide for sightseeing, I asked about the political condition of the country. He just shook his head and told us that the country's ideological struggle put its development in limbo.

I was shocked to hear from the guide that a postal address system has not been established, and that I should mail a letter to a "third house east of the church in Granada, Nicaragua," for an example.

However, San Juan del Sur, a sleepy little Pacific Coast fishing village, became the country's main seaside destination, complete with a handful of lovely hotels and a port for cruise ships according to the guide. But San Juan del Sur so far remains a laid back and charming place, whose beach is clean and mellow.

Lake Nicaragua

San Juan del Sur is, however, also an action place, offering guided horseback riding tours, zipping through the forests on a Flying Frog Canopy Tour, excellent deep-sea fishing and scuba diving. This harbor town earns its role as a Mecca for surfers, who have a choice of 14 neighboring beaches which can be reached by road or boat taxi.

The guide took us to the Lake Nicaragua, a freshwater lake which is the largest lake in Central America, and is intermittently joined by the Tipitapa River to Lake Managua.

Before construction of the Panama Canal, a stagecoach line owned by Cornelius Vanderbilt's Accessory Transit Company connected the lake with the Pacific across the low hills of the narrow Isthmus of Rivas. Plans were made to take advantage of this

Convent of San Francisco

route to build an interoceanic canal, the Nicaragua Canal, but the Panama Canal was built instead.

Some of our traveling group went to the city of Granada, which is located in the shadow of the towering Mombache Volcano. The 500-year-old city of Granada is a stunning mosaic of ornate churches, narrow streets and colorful Moorish and Andalusian style houses.

The beautiful Convent of San Francisco stands proudly as a shining example of the city's rich architectural and cultural heritage. Built in 1585, it was destroyed twice by pirates in the 17th century but rose

like a phoenix to become one of Nicaragua's most popular attractions.

Christ of Mercy

When we came back to the harbor city, our guide took us to the Christ of the Mercy, which is a colossal statue of Jesus Christ rising to a height of 134 meters. This tall statue is located high above the northernmost seawall in the bay of San Juan. At the foot of the statue is a small chapel. Information inside the chapel provides the full name of the work in Spanish along with text dating the construction to 2009.

19 Puerto Vallarta, Mexico

On March 27, 2019, we arrived in Puerto Vallarta, the last harbor before the final destination, San Pedro of Los Angele. This beautiful city is a major town for the Mexico Riviera cruise, and we have visited here many times.

We decided to walk along the Malecon, where there is a feel-good area right on the ocean front. It's a fast track to what Puerto Vallarta is all about. The colors, the sounds, and aromas, all took us under their spell and we can end up just walking around for hours, enjoying a great breakfast, lunch or dinner, eating and drinking here and there, grabbing souvenirs, shooting photos. Time just flew by, as it does when we are having fun.

El Malecon

El Malecon is now closed to vehicle traffic, so we were able to take a relaxing stroll along this sightseeing paradise walkway with great scenery, beautiful sculptures and friendly people, without having to worry about taxis, cars or buses.

This recent iteration of the classical Malecon features many more decorative plants and palm trees, that provide much-needed shade during the midday hours. All spaces have been designed with pedestrians in mind, so there are lots of places you can rest and really take time to enjoy and absorb the vibe. It is a beautiful walk along the beach in a downtown area that is full of new experiences and colorful opportunities to discover the culture, traditions and lively side of Mexico and Mexicans.

Lady of Guadalupe Church

Then we walked up to stairs to the Puerto Vallarta's Lady of Guadalupe Church, which is a city icon, it dominates Vallarta's downtown skyline and is one of the favorite symbols and landmarks of the city, in photos, shirts, logos and postcards.

As any town in the lands that were part of the Spanish conquest of America, you'll find a church, that is always placed by the main square in the village or town. Many are out of proportion to the size of the city or town, others are very simple, with almost nothing more than an altar.

Puerto Vallarta is of course no exception. The history of this important church in town is quite interesting and represents in a building the changes the town has had along the way, going from a small village all the way to a big city. In the church you'll recognize various styles, like the neoclassical in the main building and the renaissance-styled towers.

It not only is great for your souvenir photos; you'll get a glimpse of one of the most important monuments of the city and the spiritual center of the Catholics in town.

House of Richard Burton and Elizabeth Taylor

I knew the house Richard Burton bought for Elizabeth Taylor in 1964 was not far from the church, and I went up hundreds of steps up to the house, which had a big plate with the address and names of both.

The love affair of Burton and Taylor while shooting that move," Night of the Iguana" had been breaking stories every day at the time, and the whole world had to learn about the town of Puerto Vallarta and the movie ignited the town's rapid development.

Mismaloya Bay

Some of our traveling group wanted to see Mismaloya, which is located on the beach overlooking Mismaloya Bay, 12 minutes from town. On-site is Cerro de la Iguana (hill of the Iguana), location of the famous movie set where Richard Burton and Elizabeth Taylor shared their love. It's a beautiful spot to enjoy delicious seafood and marvel at beautiful sunsets.

We toured a tequila factory, Don Tadeo, near Puerto Vallarta. True tequila is only produced in Mexico, and it has deep historical roots that parallel the turbulent evolution of Mexico itself. The Spanish conquistadors were the first to distill agave, making tequila into one of the first indigenous distilled spirits in what would become North America.

Today, tequila must still be made from the cores, of the blue agave plant that only grows in a few spots in Mexico. The cores are roasted and ground, then the resulting extract will spend time fermenting. From there, the tequila is distilled and then aged to perfection in the signature toasted barrels that impart that unique rich flavor.

Epilogue

After 82 years, I've realized the simple truth that my family and friends are an integral part of my happiness. I regret that I have often, foolishly, pursued fame and money at the expense of my genuine happiness. I've also discovered joy in life when working hard to overcome challenges and adversity caused by unforeseen events, destiny, or divine providence.

I believe the remainder of my life should be devoted to the happiness of others instead of my own. I intend to maintain my physical and mental strength in order to devote myself to others, especially my wife of 57years, my three children, their spouses, and five grandchildren.

As the main part of my retirement, I am writing, reading and publishing. I enjoy tending a garden that is thriving with vegetables and citrus fruits. I also love to travel around the world with a particular fondness for the beautiful mountains and Buddhist temples in my beloved country, Korea.

Publications

The following eight books were published by an amazon.com publishing company and are available to be purchased from the amazon.com:

Dear Children (2009: ISBN# 978-0-557-14584-3)

Destiny of a Running Horse (2011: ISBN# 978-1-453-76740-5)

Traveling Stories (2013: ISBN# 978-1-475-500156-3)

여행 이야기 [Traveling Stories] (2013: ISBN# 978-1-489-59897-4

여행 이야기2 [Traveling Stories2] (2014: ISBN# 978-1-496-05479-1)

여행 이야기3 [Traveling Stories3] (2015: ISBN# 978-1-503-18517-3)

여행 이야기5 [Traveling Stories5] (2016: ISBN# 978-1-517-12352-9)

From Korea to the World (2017: ISBN# 978-1-537-42605-7)

The following books had been published before my retirement:

Mass Communication and Korea: A Global Perspective for Research,
 The Sungkok Foundation, Seoul, Korea, 1988.

Mass Media in China: Its History and Future, Iowa State University Press: Ames, Iowa, 1989.

The Rise of Asian Advertising (with Teddy Palasthira and Hung Kyu Kim), Nanam: Seoul, Korea, 1995.

장박사와 미주리 언론마피아 [Dr. Chang and Journalism Mafia] 1995 나남출판.

하이! 닥터 장 [Hi! Dr. Chang], 1997, 벽호출판.

미국을 넘으면 한국이 보인다 [Korea and America], 1988, 도서출판 이채.

미국신문의 위기와 장래 [Crisis and Future of American Newspapers] 1988나남출판.

새로운 청년을 위하여 [For Young People], 2000, 중앙 M&B.

은퇴 없는 은퇴 [Retirement without Retiring], 2001: ISBN# 978-89-960072-0-3 **03040**.

Printed in the USA
CPSIA information can be obtained
at www.ICGtesting.com
LVHW102014090823
754787LV00001B/31